1. Introduction

Cross-border flows of capital have grown rapidly in size and importance in recent decades.[1] They are an important source of capital in emerging markets and make up a significant proportion of GDP in many countries around the world. The international investment literature provides an extensive list of determinants of bilateral capital flows, ranging from geographic proximity and macroeconomic conditions to institutional factors. In this paper, we examine whether fluctuations in policy uncertainty leads to variation in foreign investment. Rodrik (1990), for example, argues that even well-meaning government effort such as liberalization or market-oriented reforms may need to take a back seat when it places the sustainability of policies into question as policy uncertainty creates incentives for foreigners to withhold investment. To date, however, there is little empirical evidence supporting the view that political uncertainty affects foreign investment.

While all investments are exposed to the risk that government policies may shift and adversely alter the expected payoffs to investors, foreign investment is burdened with additional layers of rules and regulations associated with national boundaries such as capital controls and differential tax treatments. Dixit (2011) highlights the fact that foreign direct investment (FDI) is more sensitive to the political environment than domestic investment as the foreign investor has limited protection from the host country's legal and political institutions. Foreign investments may be riskier as host governments likely view the expropriation of foreigners as more politically palatable than the expropriation of citizens. Courts in destination countries may have a bias towards domestic firms and investors in the case of disputes (Bhattacharya, Galpin and Haslem (2007)). Among the various types of international capital flows, FDI is thought to be most sensitive to policy uncertainty and institutions.

---

[1] According to UNCTAD (2009), foreign direct investment inflows worldwide grew by a factor of nearly 10 from $208 billion in 1990 to a historic high of $1,979 billion in 2007. A Coordinated Portfolio Investment Survey conducted by the International Monetary Fund (IMF) reveals that foreign portfolio investment holdings worldwide grew more than six-fold between 1997 and 2007.

The recent global financial crisis and subsequent recession has spawned a fast growing literature investigating the effects of policy uncertainty on economic activity. Cross-border flows of capital also experienced a large contraction and slow recovery.[2] A recent debate has focused on why growth in the wake of the financial crisis has been slow to recover. One of the explanations for the sluggish recovery offered by some commentators is that uncertainty about future government policy is abnormally high.[3] However, the literature has highlighted that the two empirical challenges to establishing a clear link between political uncertainty and real outcomes are first measuring political uncertainty and second identifying the causal effect of uncertainty on investment (Baker, Bloom and Davis (2012)).

To measure policy uncertainty, we employ the approach of Durnev (2010), Gao and Qi (2013), Jens (2012), Julio and Yook (2012) and Colak, Durnev and Qian (2013) and utilize the timing of elections as a measure of variation in political uncertainty. Specifically, we examine direct investment and portfolio investment flows around the timing of national elections in destination countries around the world. The outcomes of national elections are relevant to FDI decisions as they have implications for foreign capital controls, trade policy, and taxation as well as other policies that are applicable to both domestic and foreign firms such as industry regulation and fiscal policy. Changes in these policies can affect the risk and return properties of real investment. When opposing candidates in an election promote different policies, uncertainty about the election outcome implies uncertainty about what policies will be enacted after the election. There is empirical evidence supporting our assumption that political uncertainty is significantly higher around elections. Bialkowski, Gottschalk, and Wisniewski (2008) and Boutchkova et al. (2012) find that return volatility is significantly higher than normal during

---

[2]Annual global foreign direct investment inflows fell 16% in 2008, and a further 37% to $1,114 billion in 2009 before showing modest recovery in the first half of 2010 (UNCTAD (2010)). Bertaut and Pounder (2009) examine bilateral portfolio investment between the U.S. and the rest of the world and report a considerable pullback from cross-border positions during the financial crisis. As of mid-2009, the portfolio flows have yet to recover to the pre-crisis level.

[3]For example, see the Distinguished Speaker presentation by Chester Spatt at the 2009 Western Finance Association conference and comments by Ben Bernanke in the July 22, 2010 edition of the *Wall Street Journal*.

election periods around the world. Bernhard and Leblang (2006) document changes in bond yields, exchange rates, and equity volatility around elections, and show that these changes are larger when elections outcomes are close. Additionally, Baker, Bloom and Davis (2012) construct an index of policy-related economic uncertainty in the United States, and note that this index spikes upward during elections.

The second challenge in testing whether policy uncertainty depresses international investment activity is the likely endogeneity between measures of political uncertainty and economic fundamentals. As Rodrik (1991) notes, it is very difficult to find strong empirical support for uncertainty-driven predictions because political instability and uncertainty are likely endogenous to other factors that affect private investment decisions. Estimating the direction of causality between economic outcomes and policy uncertainty requires employing a variable or event that is correlated with policy uncertainty but uncorrelated with the economic conditions that drive foreign investment. Election timing is admittedly a very broad measure of political uncertainty, capturing not only possible changes in government policy but also changes in the composition of government. The timing of an election in one country is out of the control of any individual firm in another country and indeed fixed in time by constitutional rules for a large number of countries in our sample. Thus, elections around the world provide a natural experiment framework for studying the effects of policy uncertainty on FDI flows, allowing us to disentangle some of the endogeneity between economic conditions and political uncertainty. If political uncertainty is higher when changes in national leadership are more probable, elections provide some exogenous variation in policy risk over time that helps isolate the impact of policy uncertainty on FDI choices from other confounding factors. In addition, elections around the world take place at different points in time, allowing us to net out global time trends in FDI flows.

Using 184 national elections in 45 countries between January 1994 and June 2010, we examine changes in quarterly FDI flows as political uncertainty fluctuates by comparing the investment flows in the quarters leading up to the national election outcomes with those in non-election quarters. The large body of literature documenting determinants of FDI flows gives us a good benchmark empirical model to gauge abnormal changes in capital flows around the election cycle. We find clear evidence that U.S. FDI flows are significantly lower in the quarter just prior to an election outcome in the destination country. Our empirical results are consistent with the view that policy uncertainty depresses flows of private investment. The election effect remains strong when controlling for various macroeconomic and institutional factors such as GDP growth, exchange rate changes, trade openness, government stability, government expenditure, and stock market returns as well as country and time fixed effects. The baseline results suggest that the FDI flow rate falls by approximately 12% relative to non-election years, all else being equal. The magnitude of decline in the FDI rate compares to an average reduction in domestic corporate investment around election cycles of 4.8% documented by Julio and Yook (2012) and 4.5% by Jens (2012), suggesting that FDI is more sensitive to policy uncertainty than is domestic investment. To address the concern that incumbents may opportunistically time elections to maximize their chance of re-election and thereby induce a correlation between election timing and economic activity, we repeat the tests with the subsample of countries for which elections are fixed in time by electoral law. The results are similar in the subsample of elections with exogenous timing.

We also find that the election effects are stronger when the election race is close, suggesting that a higher degree of uncertainty regarding election outcomes is associated with larger drops in FDI flows in election quarters. The investment cycles are more pronounced in countries with less stable political systems and fewer checks and balances on executive authority. Election effects are smaller when the host country is more open to international trade. Election cycles in FDI flows are present, though less severe, in high income countries as well, suggesting that the depressing effects of policy uncertainty on FDI flows are not just an emerging markets phenomenon. In addition to policy risk in destination countries, we find

4

that the source country's political uncertainty affects FDI flows. Specifically, U.S. investors' FDI flows are similarly sensitive to elections abroad and to U.S. elections. FDI flows drop significantly in the quarter leading up to the U.S. election and then return to normal levels after the election resolution. This suggests that policy considerations in multiple countries are relevant for multinational firms.

A remaining challenge in the political uncertainty literature is the identification of causal effects. While the election timing alleviates many econometric concerns and it is clear that various economic activities vary over the election cycle, an unresolved issue is whether the observed effects are the result of heightened political uncertainty or whether the effects are driven by some other political mechanism, such as political business cycles (Nordhaus 1975). The political business cycle literature has highlighted the incentives of incumbent politicians to attempt to manipulate the economy to improve their re-election chances. While the political business cycle models typically predict a positive jump in economic activity prior to an election, it is possible that such attempts may crowd out private investment and lead the researcher to incorrectly conclude that uncertainty drives the result. Our identification strategy involves comparing two sets of flows into the same country in the same time period. The two sets of flows, FDI and foreign portfolio flows (FPI), have similar return properties and sensitivities to fundamentals. They differ significantly, however, with respect to the ease with which investments can be reversed, allowing us to distinguish uncertainty effects from political business cycle effects.

Irreversibility is an important feature in models of investment under uncertainty. Because investment is costly to reverse, irreversibility increases the information value of waiting to invest (Caballero (1991)), causing investment to vary negatively with fluctuations in policy uncertainty over time. The resulting prediction that the investment-uncertainty relation will be more negative for more irreversible assets has been examined in various contexts. For example, Bulan (2005) uses asset specificity at the industry level as a measure of the capital irreversibility and documents the negative investment-uncertainty relation for irreversible industries. Guiso and Parigi (1999) find more negative uncertainty-investment relation for firms with high irreversibility measured by their access to secondary markets for their capital equipment and by their comovement with other firms within an industry. Kim and Kung (2013) find a strong relationship between asset redeployability and investment sensitivity to uncertainty. In an international setting, Rajan and Marwah (1998) examine the difference in the degree of irreversibility between exports and FDI, and present a model in which the policies that are perceived as weakly credible lead firms to favor servicing foreign markets through exports rather than by undertaking FDI. FDI flows are, by definition, long-term, relationship-specific investments that are costly to reverse.[4] Caballero and Hammour (1998) point out that FDI is like investing in specific assets that ex post cannot be retrieved according to ex-ante terms of trade.

While FDI flows are typically considered relatively irreversible due to specificity, foreign portfolio investment (FPI) flows are considered to be easier to reverse (Razin, Sadka and Yuen (1998)). In our last set of tests, we incorporate this intuition and compare different flows into the same country in the same time period that have similar return properties with respect to fundamentals, but differ in their sensitivity to uncertainty. We compare relatively irreversible FDI flows to FPI flows around the election cycle. If the result is driven by fundamentals, then both flows should be affected by the election cycle. If political uncertainty is the mechanism, then we expect FDI flows to decline more than FPI flows. We find that FDI flows are sensitive to election cycles whereas FPI flows, which can be reversed at a relatively lower cost, are not sensitive to the election cycles around the world. This lends support to our primary hypothesis that policy uncertainty is driving our empirical findings and highlights the mechanism through which policy uncertainty generates the time series variation in cross-border investment flows.

---

[4]Balance of Payments Manual, fifth edition (IMF, 1993).

Our empirical predictions are drawn from established theoretical literature related to the effects of political uncertainty. Rodrik (1991) models private foreign investment choices in a setting with policy uncertainty. In his model, foreign investors hold back on investing until a large amount of uncertainty regarding the success of political reform is resolved. Chen and Funke (2003) also model FDI decisions in the face of policy uncertainty and generate similar predictions. In this context, policy uncertainty has a negative effect on private investment when the investment is at least partially irreversible. The impact on investment in this setting is significant. Rodrik demonstrates that under reasonable assumptions even a 10 percent probability of policy reversal requires an investment subsidy of 7.5 percentage points to offset its adverse effects on investment. Thus, policy uncertainty acts like a tax on investment. The intuition is similar in general models of investment under uncertainty, including Bernanke (1983) and Bloom, Bond, and Van Reenen (2007), that the value of waiting increases when uncertainty related to changes in government policy is high. Pindyck and Solimano (1993) is another example of this literature in which the uncertainty brought about by political factors leads firms to choose lower levels of investment expenditures.

Our paper contributes to two important sets of literature. First, the FDI literature provides an extensive list of the determinants of FDI including macroeconomic variables such as GDP and exchange rate fluctuations, institutional quality, and firm-level cost considerations[5]. A number of studies examine the implication of political institutions for FDI. Wei (2000) documents that corruption in the recipient country substantially reduces FDI inflows. Singh and Jun (1995) document that FDI flows are especially sensitive to political risk in countries that have historically attracted high FDI flows. Daude and Fratzscher (2008) document that FPI is more sensitive to institutional factors than FDI. Desai et al. (2008) and Desai et al. (2004) document that political risk affects the variability of foreign affiliates' returns as well as the capital structure decisions of both the parent and affiliates of multinational firms. We depart

---

[5]See section 3.4 for more discussion of FDI determinants.

from this strand of literature in that we focus on uncertainty surrounding policy rather than policy per se, and investigate whether perceived policy shifts affect the expected payoff to investment. In related work, Wei (1997) documents that uncertainty regarding corruption has important negative effects on FDI decisions. Hermes and Lensink (2001) document that policy uncertainty has a positive impact on the outflow of domestic capital. Our study has a broad application in that, while institutional variables such as corruption and investor protection have applications mainly in less developed countries, policy uncertainty is an important concern for developed countries as well.

Our paper also contributes to the recent literature focusing on the interaction between political change and finance. Kim, Pantzalis, and Park (2012) investigate the impact of variation in political geography brought on the outcomes of mid-term elections and find a significant effect on returns. Gao and Qi (2013) show that the uncertainty around gubernatorial elections in the U.S. is reflected in higher offering yields of municipal bonds. Durnev (2010) examines firm investment around national elections in an international setting and finds that investment is less sensitive to stock prices in election years. Julio and Yook (2012) find that corporate investment rates drop by an average of around 5% in the pre-election period for a sample of 48 countries. Our paper complements these papers and shows how policy uncertainty affects cross-border capital flows. We also contribute to the literature focused on the causes of the sluggish recovery following the financial crisis. Baker, Bloom, and Davis (2012) construct an index of economic policy uncertainty and find evidence consistent with the hypothesis that abnormally high levels of policy uncertainty is responsible for a significant amount of unemployment and slow growth. While we do not address the recession directly, our results suggest that the link between policy uncertainty and investment is likely a causal one. Our results also support the use of election timing as a proxy variable for fluctuations in political uncertainty over time.

2. Data Description

2.1. Cross-Border Investment Data

This study considers investments abroad by U.S. investors in the form of foreign direct investment and foreign portfolio investment between 1994 and June 2010. The sample includes information on direct investment to 43 countries and portfolio investment to 44 countries. The FDI data set is drawn from the Survey of U.S. Direct Investment Abroad conducted by the U.S. Bureau of Economic Analysis. U.S. direct investment abroad is defined as ownership by a U.S. investor of at least 10 percent of a foreign business. The direct investor is known as a U.S. parent and the U.S.-owned foreign business is known as a foreign affiliate. FDI flows capture the funds that U.S. parents provide to their foreign affiliates including equity investment, intra-company loans and reinvested earnings. FDI flows (reported in U.S. dollars) are measured on a quarterly frequency, which allows us to track the changes in the flows around the election cycles that cannot be captured in lower-frequency data such as annual data provided by UNCTAD. FDI positions, which are stocks and cumulative, are reported annually and measure the total outstanding level of U.S. direct investment abroad at year-end. The foreign portfolio investment (FPI) data contain information on net purchases of long-term foreign securities, both debt and equities, by U.S. residents. We use Bertaut and Tryon's (2007) estimates of monthly bilateral FPI flows and positions data maintained by the Federal Reserve. Bertaut and Tryon adjust the FPI data collected by the Treasury International Capital (TIC) reporting system to alleviate the biases pointed out by previous studies.[6] The resulting estimates are consistent with various officially reported data (Curcuru, Thomas, Warnock and Wongswan (2011)).

---

[6]Previous studies suggest that the so-called TIC data need adjustments regarding acquisitions of equity through stock swaps, principal repayment flows on asset-backed corporate securities, and financial center biases, among others. (Chuhan, Claessens, and Mamingi (1998), Griever, Lee, and Warnock (2001), Thomas, Warnock, Wongswan (2004), Warnock and Cleaver (2003), and Warnock and Warnock (2005))

Panel A of Table 1 summarizes annual FDI and FPI flows by country (in $US millions). Note that quarterly FDI flows and monthly FPI flows are annualized to generate comparable summary statistics. The average annual FDI flows range from a low of $65 million in Greece to a high of $24 billion to the United Kingdom and the Netherlands. FPI is made up of foreign portfolio equity investment (FPEI) and foreign portfolio debt investment (FPDI). The highest average annual FPI flow is $43.6 billion to the United Kingdom with $24.8 billion in equity investment and $18.8 billion in debt investment while the lowest is –$2.1 billion to Singapore with $311 million in equity investment and –$2.4 billion in debt investment. The negative figure indicates that U.S. investors sold more Singaporean debt securities than they purchased the securities during the sample period.

2.2. Election Data

Our measure for variation in policy uncertainty is the timing of national elections held between January 1994 and June 2010. The detailed election information is obtained from a variety of sources. The primary source for election and regime change data is the Polity IV database maintained by the Center for International Development and Conflict Management at the University of Maryland. This database contains annual information on the regime and authority characteristics of all independent states with total populations greater than 500,000. The second major source of information is the World Bank Database of Political Institutions. This source provides information about electoral rules and the classification of political platforms for the elected leaders and candidates. We supplement the election data with various internet sources[7] for cases in which the election information is missing from the Polity IV database or the Database of Political Institutions.

---

[7]Other internet sources include http://www.cidcm.umd.edu/polity/data/, http://www.binghamton.edu/cdp/era/searchera html, and http://www.electionresources.org/.

We collect the election data for the U.S. and 44 destination countries for which the data on bilateral investment with the U.S. are available. We focus on elections in which the choice of national leader or executive authority is made. We include presidential elections for countries with presidential systems, and legislative elections for countries with parliamentary systems. Some countries have a hybrid system combining elements of both parliamentary and presidential democracy; a president and a prime minister coexist with both presidential and legislative elections held nationally. In such cases, the constitutional framework and practice are examined in greater detail to understand how executive power is divided between the two leaders, and the election associated with the leader who exerts more power over executive decisions is selected for the study. The data include 31 countries with legislative elections and 14 countries with presidential elections, resulting in total of 184 national elections for our sample period.

An important characteristic of national elections is whether the timing of elections is exogenously specified by electoral law. Our identification assumption is that the timing of national elections is correlated with changes in policy uncertainty but uncorrelated with other determinants of FDI flows. There may be some concern that the timing of elections is a function of economic conditions in a recipient country. In some electoral systems a government can be dissolved before the expiry of its full term for various reasons and an election is then normally called to form a new government. The potential correlation between election timing and economic conditions may confound the effect of policy uncertainty on FDI flows. For example, Ito (1990) shows that the timing of Japanese general elections is consistent with opportunistic timing of incumbents calling elections when economic conditions are good. While opportunistic election timing is likely to bias against the finding dampened FDI flows in election periods, we classify countries as having either exogenous timing or endogenous timing to address the potential endogeneity. All countries with a record of early elections are classified as having endogenous timing. All presidential elections in the sample are held on a fixed basis and as such are classified as having exogenous timing. For the remaining countries, we examine electoral laws and practices as well as the timing classification by Alesina, Cohen, and Roubini (1992).[8] Our classification procedure results in 19 countries with fixed election timing and 26 countries with flexible timing.

Panel A of Table 2 summarizes the election data. For the countries in our sample, we observe an election in each country every 16.4 quarters on average. The average length of term for elected national leaders in our sample is 4.4 years. Of all the elections in the sample, 73.6% take place in parliamentary systems. 45.3% of the elections in our sample are fixed in time by electoral law and hence outside the control of incumbent politicians. The remaining elections are in systems in which there is a mechanism for calling elections prior to the expiry of the term of the government. We observe frequent turnover in leadership, with 56.4% of the elections resulting in a change in the government head and 48.9% resulting in a change in the ruling party. There is a large amount of dispersion in the magnitudes in margin of victory across elections. On average, the winner received 41.7% of the vote, compared to 28.6% for the runner-up.

2.3. Country Characteristics

The country-level control variables are motivated by prior research that examine the determinants of cross-border capital flows.[9] Following the literature, we employ several variables that capture macroeconomic and institutional characteristics of the destination country. The World Bank database is our primary source for the macroeconomic variables including real per capita GDP, government spending, exports, and imports. We also obtain monthly exchange rate data from IMF International Financial Statistics. Monthly returns on countries' stock market indices are drawn from Datastream and Bloomberg. Data on monthly government sta-

---

[8]Alesina, Cohen, and Roubini (1992) classify the timing of elections as exogenous or endogenous for 18 developed countries.

[9]See, for example, Albuquerque, Loayza, and Serven (2005), Froot and Stein (1991), and Blonigen (1997)

bility ratings are from Political Risk Service's International Country Risk Guide (ICRG). The government stability index assigns numbers between 0 and 12, where higher values indicate more stable governments. The government stability index is time-varying and assesses the government's ability to carry out its declared programs and its ability to stay in office.

We obtain an annual measure of the degree of checks and balances for each political system in our sample from the Database of Political Institutions. The metric is intended to capture the number of decision makers whose agreement is necessary for the approval of policy changes. It is calculated as the number of veto players in the political system at a given point in time based on the prevailing electoral rules and laws. It also takes into account whether the executive and legislative branches of government are controlled by the same party, which effectively reduces the checks and balances relative to having different parties controlling separate branches of government. In presidential systems, the count is increased by one for the president and increased by one for each additional legislative body. For parliamentary systems, the count is increased by one for the prime minister and increased by the number of parties included in the governing coalition. The number is reduced if the party of the executive is the same as the largest party in any particular chamber of government. In our empirical analysis, the checks and balances measure provides us with variation, both within and across countries, in the degree to which policy changes are likely following a given election.

Panel B of Table 2 summarizes the characteristics of 44 destination countries. For our sample, the average government stability rating is 7.82. GDP per capita has a mean value of $9,183 per year and the median of $3,273. The average government consumption is 16% of GDP and the average monthly return on stock market indices is 1%. Trade openness, measured as the sum of exports and imports scaled by GDP, averages 79% of GDP across countries.

3. Empirical Results

This section tests the hypothesis that increased uncertainty around national elections reduces FDI flows. The empirical analysis exploits the timing of national elections around the world to identify variation in policy uncertainty. We begin by discussing how we measure FDI flows. We then turn to a regression analysis to measure the impact of policy uncertainty on FDI flows. We then explore variation across countries and elections and finish with an examination of foreign portfolio investment flows around election cycles.

3.1. Measuring FDI Flows

Following the literature, we scale the flows or use a variance stabilizing transformation, as described below. The first measure is the growth in the stock of FDI, similar to the measure employed by Baker, Foley and Wurgler (2009). This measure is the ratio of the U.S. FDI flows to country j in quarter t to the cumulative U.S. FDI position in country j at the end of quarter $t-1$, as follows:

$$FDI/Position_{jt} = \frac{FDI_t^{US \to j}}{Position_{t-1}^{US \to j}},$$

where J is the number of countries in our sample. The second measure captures the U.S. FDI flows to country j during quarter t as a proportion of total U.S. FDI flows around the world in quarter $t-1$. That is,

$$FDI/Total_{jt} = \frac{FDI_t^{US \to j}}{\sum_{j=1}^{J} FDI_{t-1}^{US \to j}}.$$

14

This measure is intended to capture the share of total FDI flows going to each destination country in our sample. The measure is similar in spirit to that employed by Dewenter (1995) who scales cross-border M&A flows into the U.S. by U.S. domestic acquisition activity. The third measure we employ, similar to that used by Froot and Stein (1991), is the U.S. FDI flows to a recipient country in a given quarter scaled by the lagged GDP of the recipient country. The final measure is a variation of the log transformation used by Busse and Hefeker (2007). Since the FDI flows are measured on a net basis, some country-quarter observations have negative values. To preserve the observations with negative values, Busse and Hefeker (2007) used the transformation

$$ln\left(FDI_{jt} + \sqrt{(FDI_{jt}^2 + 1)}\right).$$

For robustness, we run all regressions with each of the four measures of FDI flows.

We construct the corresponding four measures for foreign portfolio investment (FPI) flows. Panel B of Table 1 presents the summary statistics for raw FDI and FPI flows, flows to GDP, flows to position, and the log transform of Busse and Hefeker (2007). Foreign portfolio equity investment (FPEI) flows and foreign portfolio debt investment (FPDI) flows are reported separately. FDI flows are, on average, somewhat larger than FPI flows, while FPI flows display more time-series variation.

3.2. Measuring Policy Uncertainty

As noted by Rodrik (1991), a major obstacle to identifying a link between policy uncertainty and changes in capital flows is the availability of an adequate proxy for variation in uncertainty due to difficulties in measurement and possible endogeneity. Major events that create policy uncertainty are likely correlated with economic conditions, making it difficult to establish the direction of causality between changes in uncertainty and changes in capital flows. To deal with this challenge, we employ the identification strategy of Julio and Yook

15

(2012) and Durnev (2010) and use the timing of national elections around the world as a measure of variation in political uncertainty. Specifically, we create an election timing dummy variable equal to one in quarter t if the election occurs in the second half of quarter t or in the first half of quarter $t+1$.[10] We use election timing as a proxy for variation in political uncertainty of the destination country as the timing of elections is out of the control of the U.S. firms and investors and indeed for a large part of our sample the timing of elections is fixed by electoral law and hence independent of general economic conditions.

The identification strategy requires that political uncertainty is indeed higher during election periods. A growing literature has documented that the probability of policy changes does appear to increase around elections. Several papers have found such evidence in financial markets. Bialkowski, Gottschalk, and Wisniewski (2008) and Boutchkova et al. (2012) find that volatility is significantly higher than normal during election periods around the world. Boutchkova et al. (2012) document that equity return volatility is higher around elections in politically sensitive industries. Bernhard and Leblang (2006) document changes in bond yields, exchange rates, and equity volatility around elections, and show that these changes are larger during close elections. More recently, Baker, Bloom and Davis (2012) construct an index of economic policy uncertainty in the United States composed of news media references to policy uncertainty, future expiration of federal tax code provisions, and forecaster disagreement over inflation and government purchases. Their index spikes upward around U.S. presidential elections, consistent with the premise that political uncertainty is higher in election periods.

---

[10]The results are robust to different cutoff points for the election timing dummy.

3.3. FDI Flows around Elections

As a first step, we examine variation in FDI flows from the U.S. to destination countries around election dates by estimating the specification

$$FDI_{jt} = \gamma_j + \delta_t + \sum_{k=-2}^{2} \beta_k Election_{j,t+k} + \varepsilon_{jt}, \qquad (1)$$

where γ_j captures country fixed effects and δ_t time fixed effects of a quarterly frequency. We construct an election dummy variable to capture the quarter leading up to the election. The election variable is set equal to one if a national election is held in the second half of a given quarter or in the first half of the next quarter, and zero otherwise. Four additional dummy variables are included to examine possible changes in FDI flows in the two quarters preceding the election quarter and the two quarters just following the election. The specification in (1) is intended to capture within-country variation in FDI flows around the election cycle, with no additional control variables aside from the fixed effects. Standard errors are clustered at the country level.

Table 3 reports the estimation results for specification (1). Consistent with the hypothesis that policy uncertainty has a depressing effect on FDI, the U.S. FDI flows to a destination country are lower in quarters in which a national election is held in the destination country. The effect is economically and statistically significant. The coefficient for the specification using FDI/Position as the dependent variable suggests that FDI flows from the U.S. to a recipient country are 11.9% lower in election quarters relative to the country mean annual rate of FDI flows. The signs and magnitudes for the other transformations of FDI flows yield similar results.

3.4. Including Determinants of FDI Flows

We next introduce to our specification various time-varying country characteristics that can potentially affect FDI flows[11]. GDP per capita, for example, is expected to control for the effect of a host country's wealth on FDI decisions. Higher volatility in GDP growth or in real exchange rates is associated with macroeconomic instability, which is considered to drive away FDI. Changes in the real exchange rate affect the relative wealth levels of foreign and domestic investors and may lead to changes in investors' actual relative purchasing power (Froot and Stein (1991) and Klein and Rosengren (1994)). Tax is also an important consideration for the choice of FDI location (Hines and Rice (1994)) because higher taxes generally discourage private investment. Further, tax influences the capital structure decision and the choice between internal and external financing for multinational firms (Desai et al. (2004)). Stock market valuation may drive FDI, especially cross-border mergers and acquisitions (Baker, Foley, and Wurgler (2009)). Undervaluation in the host-country stock market may present an attractive investment opportunity for international investors (Shleifer and Vishny (1992), Krugman (1998), and Aguiar and Gopinath (2005)). Also, the overvalued market of the source country may provide multinational firms with relatively low-cost funding for overseas investment (Shleifer and Vishny (2003)). Trade openness may influence FDI decisions in two opposite manners. Larger openness may further facilitate FDI if foreign production requires parent firms to supply production parts to their affiliates in host countries. Also, if a firm expects its production presence in a foreign market with one product to generate demand for other products of the firm, larger trade openness may promote FDI (Lipsey and Weiss (1984)). On the other hand, if multinationals have to choose between foreign production and exports based on considerations on tariffs, transport costs, and location advantages (Markusen (1995)), smaller trade openness may lead to higher FDI.

---

[11]See Albuquerque, Loayza, and Serven (2005) and Daude and Fratzscher (2008) for an extensive list of potential determinants of cross-border investment.

In addition to the time-varying country characteristics, we also include country fixed effects to control for time-invariant country characteristics associated with FDI decisions. Examples of such country characteristics include geographic and language proximity and legal origin (Daude and Fratzscher (2008)). Capital controls may also have a direct or indirect implication on FDI by influencing the foreign affiliates' borrowing environments or repatriation decisions (Desai et al. (2006)), or by influencing the volatility of macroeconomic conditions (Aizenman (2003), Bekaert, Harvey, and Lundblad (2006)). The liberalization dummy variable, a common measure of capital control, is largely time-invariant for our sample period because all countries in our sample with one exception have already been liberalized prior to the beginning of our sample period.[12]

We estimate the regression

$$FDI_{jt} = \gamma_j + \delta_t + \sum_{k=-2}^{2} \beta_k Election_{j,t+k} + \mathbf{X}'\theta + \varepsilon_{jt}, \tag{2}$$

where X is a vector of control variables, which include GDP per capita, GDP growth, volatility of GDP growth, the ICRG government stability ratings, government consumption as a proportion of GDP, lagged stock market returns and volatility, changes in exchange rates, exchange rate volatility, and trade openness of the recipient country. Country and time (quarterly frequency) fixed effects are included in each specification. The coefficient on the election dummy variable can be interpreted as the difference in the within-country conditional mean FDI rate, controlling for the other determinants of FDI flows.

Table 4 reports the results of the FDI regressions controlling for known determinants of FDI. The inclusion of country control variables does not change the economic magnitude of the election effects. Controlling for country characteristics, we find that FDI flows from the

---

[12]We cross-check our sample countries against the liberalization date provided by Bekaert and Harvey (2000) and Campbell R. Harvey's website. Among 38 sample countries for which the liberalization date information is available, only one country liberalized its financial market after 1994 (South Africa in 1996).

U.S. to other countries decline by 11.2% in an election quarter relative to non-election quarters. The reduction in FDI flows in the quarter leading up to the election is both statistically and economically significant. The control variables exhibit signs consistent with those documented by extant studies. GDP growth, which measures improvements in overall productivity as reflected in economic growth, has a positive sign across the board as predicted. The positive sign on trade openness suggests that larger trade openness serves to attract FDI into the recipient country. This is consistent with the previous country-level studies documenting net complementarity effects between exports and FDI[13]. GDP growth volatility shows negative association with FDI inflows as predicted, but the result is not statistically strong. Exchange rate volatility is insignificant in all four regressions. This may be because our sample consists of both developed and less-developed countries while macroeconomic instability is an important concern primarily in less-developed economies. Previous-quarter market return is significant in only one case, suggesting that the association between FDI flows and local market valuation is rather weak for our sample. An increase in government expenditures is expected to act as a deterrent for FDI inflows as increased government spending funded by higher taxation is likely to discourage private investment. However, the results show that the ratio of government expenditure to GDP is insignificant except for one case. Finally, changes in real exchange rates is insignificant. This is consistent with the empirical literature documenting that the effect of changes in the exchange rate on FDI is unclear (see Blonigen (1997) for literature review).

3.5. Domestic and Foreign Sources of Uncertainty

Firms and investors are exposed to two sources of policy uncertainty in a cross-border setting, that of the home country and that of the destination country. In this section, we

---

[13]While little evidence of substitution effects is found on the aggregate level, some evidence is documented in less aggregate data (Blonigen (2001)).

augment the empirical specification and include the U.S. elections to estimate possible effects of source country elections on FDI flows. We estimate the regression

$$FDI_{jt} = \gamma_j + \delta_t + \sum_{k=-2}^{2} \beta_k Election_{j,t+k} + \sum_{l=-2}^{2} \delta_l Election_{US,t+l} + X'\theta + \varepsilon_{jt}, \qquad (3)$$

where j denotes country and t indexes time. We construct additional dummy variables designed to capture the U.S. election effects in the quarter leading up to the election as well as the two quarters before and after the election quarter. As before, we include the election dummies for the destination countries and control variables. Year fixed effects are included to control for global trends in FDI. Note that time fixed effects of a quarterly frequency are replaced by year fixed effects whenever U.S. election dummies are included in the regressions. Because all flows in our sample originate from the US, The US election effects are harder to identify than the destination country effects in which different countries have elections in different quarters.

Table 5 reports the estimation results for the specification including the U.S. election dummies. To save space, we do not report the coefficients for the control variables and the election dummies for $t \pm 2$. As before, we find that U.S. FDI flows to a destination country are lower in country-quarters in which the country holds a national election, controlling for changes in the economic environment. The economic magnitude is considerable. The results suggest that, controlling for country-level characteristics and the timing of U.S. elections, FDI flows as a percentage of cumulative FDI stock in the given recipient country drop by 12% in the quarter leading up to a national election in the recipient country. We also observe that FDI flows originating from the U.S. tend to be lower in general during U.S. elections, suggesting that policy uncertainty in the source country depresses flows to host countries until the source country's electoral uncertainty is resolved. Taken together, the results suggest that firms and investors respond to both foreign and domestic sources of political uncertainty.

3.6. Exogenous vs. Endogenous Election Timing

One concern with the above analysis is that, for some countries in our sample, national elections may be called early by the national leader or legislative body. Early elections raise a possibility that election timing may be correlated with economic conditions and cause a bias in our estimates of the election effects. While such correlation does not appear to be generally observed[14] in the literature, there is some evidence for such correlation in Japan. Ito (1990) finds that elections in Japan are held in periods of economic expansion, suggesting opportunistic behavior of the incumbent politicians. In our sample, we find that within-country GDP growth is, on average, 1.96% higher in the period just before an election in countries that have flexibility over election timing, while we find no statistical difference in growth rates around the election cycle for countries with fixed election timing[15]. Higher GDP growth around the election cycle is consistent with either opportunistic timing or a reluctance to call elections when growth is relatively low. We note, however, that the results in Table 4 show that FDI flows are strongly pro-cyclical and hence the possible opportunistic behavior of incumbents is likely to act as a bias against finding a negative effect attributable to electoral uncertainty. To address the concern that FDI flows may be confounded with strategic election timing, we estimate the FDI regressions for the subsample of countries for which the timing of elections is fixed in time by electoral law and hence orthogonal to the business cycle.

Table 6 reports the results for the subsample with exogenous election timing. For brevity, we have only reported the coefficients for the election dummy variables, although the country

---

[14]Alesina, Cohen, and Roubini (1992) examine 14 OECD countries with flexible election timing and find that such an association between election timing and economic conditions is not present in any of those countries excluding Japan.

[15]Specifically, we estimate the regression

$$\text{GDP growth}_{jt} = \alpha_j + \gamma_t + \beta Election_{jt} + \varepsilon_{jt},$$

where α_j is a country fixed effect and γ_t is a year/quarter fixed effect. We estimate the regression separately for countries with an option to call an early election and for those countries with fixed election time. The coefficient β captures the within-country difference in GDP growth between election and non-election quarters. Results are available upon request.

controls were included in the regression. The main results are present in the countries for which election timing is fixed. The magnitude of the coefficients for elections in both destination countries and the U.S. are similar to that for the full sample. FDI flows to countries holding an election in a particular quarter drop by 9.5% compared to non-election years in the exogenous election sample. This confirms that our results are not driven by factors correlated with the opportunistic timing of elections.

3.7. Variation in Electoral Uncertainty: Close Elections

The Rodrik (1991) model suggests that the reluctance to invest in a recipient country will be higher when the country has a higher degree of uncertainty over future policy. To the extent that different candidates have different policy preferences, election uncertainty translates into policy uncertainty when the outcome is uncertain. In some cases, election outcomes are predicted with a great deal of confidence prior to the election day. Singapore, for example, has not experienced a change in the ruling party for many decades. However, some elections are characterized by very close races in which the outcome is highly uncertain until the day of the election. In this section, we investigate variation in electoral uncertainty by using election vote turnouts as a proxy for election uncertainty before the revelation of the election outcome. We construct a dummy variable equal to one if the margin of victory for a given election is in the lowest quartile of the sample distribution of victory margins. In our sample, the 25th percentile for the margin of victory is 7.1%. We then interact the close election indicator with the election dummy. We also construct an indicator variable to capture elections with wide victory margins and therefore likely to be associated with less uncertainty. We set a dummy variable equal to one if the margin of victory for a given election is in the highest quartile of the distribution. We include this dummy in some specifications to capture whether elections with more certain outcomes also create cycles in FDI flows.

23

Table 7 reports the results of the specification with the close election interaction. For the sake of brevity, we report only the regressions with the FDI/position variable as the left hand side variable. The first two columns report the estimates for the full sample of countries and the last two columns report the results for only the countries with exogenous election timing. The interaction term for close margins of victory is statistically significant in all four regressions. This finding suggests that cycles in FDI flows around national elections have a larger magnitude when the uncertainty regarding the election outcome is higher. This result is in line with Rodrik (1991), which predicts the effect of policy uncertainty is increasing in the likelihood of policy change. This result also strengthens the interpretation that the patterns we are finding in the data are related to policy uncertainty and not likely related to any other underlying mechanism. The coefficient on the wide margin of victory interaction term is positive and statistically insignificant for both the full and exogenous timing samples. The combined results suggest that declines in FDI are largest when the margin of victory is very tight and negligible when margins of victory are wide.

3.8. Variation Across Countries

In this section, we investigate the interaction between election effects and the factors that capture the potential likelihood and magnitude of policy shifts after elections. The prediction is that countries that are more susceptible to policy reversals will experience larger election cycles in FDI flows. We examine variation along four dimensions. First, we look at differences in ICRG government stability ratings. Second, we examine differences in the degree of checks and balances on executive authority, based on counts of the number of veto players within a political system at any point in time as measured by the World Bank. Third, we sort countries according to World Bank's development index, based on the idea that less developed countries may be more exposed to policy uncertainty compared to wealthier countries. Finally, we

24

examine whether the degree of trade openness affects the sensitivity of FDI to a host country's political cycles.

We estimate the regression

$$FDI_{jt} = \gamma_j + \delta_t + \alpha_1 \cdot Z_{jt} + \alpha_2 \cdot Z_{jt} \cdot Election_{jt} + \sum_{k=-2}^{2} \beta_k Election_{j,t+k} + \mathbf{X}'\theta + \varepsilon_{jt},$$

where Z_{jt} is a time-varying country characteristic intended to capture differences in the propensity for large policy changes after elections. Table 8 reports the results of the FDI regressions including the interaction terms with the four factors listed above. To save space, we only report election dummy variables and the interaction terms. We run regressions using all four FDI measures but only report results using the FDI/position variable. The first column reports the results including an interaction between the election dummy variable and ICRG government stability ratings. The point estimate of the interaction term is positive and significant.[16] While the statistical evidence is not overwhelming, it is consistent with the view that election effects in countries with more stable governments (higher ICRG rating) are mitigated relative to countries with less stable political systems. This suggests that policy uncertainty is more material in countries in which governments are less stable.

Column 2 of Table 8 presents the results with an interaction term between checks and balances and the election dummy. The coefficient on the interaction term has the sign as predicted though not significant. The regressions using the other FDI measures (unreported) produce the same sign with statistical significance. The results suggest that the effect of policy uncertainty is less severe in countries where the power of the national leader is relatively restricted in terms of making policy changes after taking office. Electoral uncertainty, therefore, appears to have larger effects on FDI flows when election outcomes may lead to relatively unchecked policy changes by the national leader.

---

[16]Regressions using other FDI measures produce similar results.

Column 3 of Table 8 reports the results of the regression that includes a high-income interaction term with the election dummy. A high-income dummy is set equal to one if a country is classified as a high-income country in a given year by World Bank. World Bank's development classification is based on the country's gross national income (GNI) each year. Somewhat surprisingly, we find that election effects on FDI flows are not significantly different between high and low-income countries, suggesting that policy uncertainty is not limited to emerging markets and less developed countries but has implications in developed countries as well. Even relatively well-developed countries experience cycles in FDI flows around election time. The results remain similar when the other FDI measures are employed (unreported). Alternatively, we repeat the test using GDP per capita and find similar results.[17]

Column 4 reports the results including an interaction between the election dummy variable and trade openness dummy variable. The coefficient on the interaction term is positive and significant, suggesting that when an economy is open to international trade, FDI decisions are less sensitive to local political environment. This is consistent with the extant studies documenting that when an economy is more open, capital flows are less correlated with a country's institutional quality. Albuquerque, Loayza, and Serven (2005) show that FDI is increasingly more dependent on global factors and less dependent on country-specific factors, suggesting that increased market integration leads to a greater role of global risk factors. Examining industry-level trade openness, Giovanni and Levchenko (2009) show that a sector that is more open to international trade is less correlated with domestic economic cycles. In a related vein, Fratzscher and Imbs (2009) and Ju and Wei (2010) examine how financial openness interacts with a country's institutional quality and show that the sensitivity of FDI to institutional factors depends on the degree of the country's financial openness.

---

[17]We set a country-quarter to one if the GDP per capita in a given country-quarter is above the median of the distribution and to zero otherwise. We also simply interact GDP per capita with the election dummy and find similar results.

3.9. Additional Robustness

We performed several robustness tests to check the consistency of our results. In results not reported here[18], we perform the following robustness tests: (1) we use raw FDI flows and the natural log of FDI flows as the dependent variable; (2) we cluster standard errors at the yearly and quarterly level rather than at the country level; (3) we include additional control variables, such as volatility of terms of trade and lead and contemporaneous values of stock returns; and (4) we estimate the FDI regressions on a country-by-country basis and take the average of the coefficients across the country regressions to make inferences; and (5) we consider only elections in which the incumbent national leader is not running for re-election. In every case listed above, the results are similar to those reported in the tables.

4. Policy Uncertainty and Irreversibility

In this section we provide evidence that the negative relationship between FDI flows and election timing reflects increased political uncertainty rather than some other election related mechanism. The political uncertainty literature has documented election effects on corporate investment (Durnev (2010), Julio and Yook (2012), Jens (2012)), borrowing costs (Gao and Qi (2013), and the IPO decision (Colak, Durnev and Qian (2013)). An unresolved question is whether election timing captures uncertainty or whether some other type of political mechanism is causing the observed relationships. For example, opportunistic models of political business cycles (PBC), beginning with Nordhaus (1975), incumbents attempt to manipulate fiscal and monetary policy to increase the probability of re-election. While opportunistic PBC models typically predict an increase in economic activity prior to an election, it is possible that FDI flows may decline because actions to stimulate the economy prior to the election may crowd out private investment. Julio and Yook (2012) show that government spending, money

---

[18]Available from the authors upon request

27

supply, interest rates and inflation do not vary across the election cycle in a similar sample of countries. However, it is possible that other, unobservable political activities near election time could have some effect on FDI flows.

Our identification strategy allows us to disentangle uncertainty effects from other mechanism by comparing two sets of flows into the same country and same time period that have different sensitivities to uncertainty but otherwise share the same return properties. Specifically, we compare FDI and FPI flows (both equity and debt) around the election cycle. The investment under uncertainty literature such as Bernanke (1983) and Rodrik (1991), among others, shows that irreversibility of investment generates an incentive to wait when uncertainty is high. When capital investment is costly to undo, investment decisions become very sensitive to the information environment, and firms and individuals have a strong incentive to wait for some degree of uncertainty to unravel before committing to investment projects. To the extent that government policy choices are relevant to expected payoffs for investment, irreversible investment will be sensitive to the policy uncertainty, as in Rodrik (1991). Empirically, Guiso and Parigi (1999) show that uncertainty has a stronger effect on firms that cannot easily resell capital equipment in secondary markets and Kim and Kung (2013) show that firms with relatively less asset redeployability decrease investment more when uncertainty is high.

FDI flows are, by definition, long-term, relationship-based investments. The IMF defines FDI as follows:

> The BPM5[19] defines FDI as a category of international investment that reflects the objective of a resident in one economy (the direct investor) obtaining a lasting interest in an enterprise resident in another economy (the direct investment enterprise). The lasting interest implies the existence of a long-term relationship between the direct investor and the direct investment enterprise, and a significant

---

[19]Balance of Payments Manual, fifth edition (IMF, 1993).

degree of influence by the investor on the management of the enterprise. A direct investment relationship is established when the direct investor has acquired 10 percent or more of the ordinary shares or voting power of an enterprise abroad.

Caballero and Hammour (1998) classify FDI as relationship-specific and argue that the specificity reduces the flexibility of decisions. While FDI flows are typically considered relatively irreversible due to specificity, FPI flows are considered to be easier to reverse (Razin, Sadka and Yuen (1998)). Comparing different types of international equity investments, Goldstein and Razin (2006) argue that FDI is more costly to reverse than FPI if investors faced with liquidity shocks need to sell their investments before maturity. Because direct investors who act effectively as managers of firms are more informed than portfolio investors, they would be forced to sell at a lower price that reflects the discount for information asymmetry. Thus, our identification strategy compares two sets of equity flows into the same country that have similar sensitivity to the macroeconomic environment but differ with respect to the degree of reversibility and hence sensitivity to political uncertainty.

To compare the effects of election timing on FDI and FPI flows, we estimate the system

$$FDI_{jt} = \gamma_j + \delta_t + \sum_{k=-2}^{2} \beta_k Election_{j,t+k} + \sum_{l=-2}^{2} \delta_l Election_{US,t+l} + \mathbf{X}'\theta + \varepsilon_{\mathbf{jt}} \qquad (4)$$

$$FPI_{jt} = \gamma'_j + \delta'_t + \sum_{k=-2}^{2} \beta'_k Election_{j,t+k} + \sum_{l=-2}^{2} \delta'_l Election_{US,t+l} + \mathbf{X}'\eta + v_{\mathbf{jt}},$$

where *FPI* represents foreign portfolio equity investments (FPEI), foreign portfolio debt investments (FPDI), or the sum of debt and equity investment flows. The right-hand-side variables include election dummy variables for both the destination and source countries and a collection of control variables as defined previously. Since both FDI and FPI share similar determinants, we estimate the system using seemingly unrelated regression estimation. The estimation procedure also allows us to test differences in coefficients across equations.

Table 9 reports the estimation results for the seemingly unrelated regressions. The first column reports the coefficients from the FDI regression. As with the previous results, FDI flows are significantly lower in the pre-election period. The following three columns report the estimates for the equity FPI, debt FPI, and combined FPI flows. The table shows that there are no significant changes in FPI flows across the election cycle for either equity or debt flows. The difference in coefficients on the election indicator variable between FDI and equity FPI flows is significantly different at the 1% level. The coefficients on the election indicator are indistinguishable from zero also for the debt flows and total FPI flows. The sensitivity of FDI to the election cycle and the absence of an effect for FPI flows suggests that the underlying mechanism driving the pre-election declines in FDI flows is heightened political uncertainty prior to the election outcome.

5. Conclusion

In this paper, we examine the relationship between cross-border flows of capital and uncertainty over future government policy. Using the timing of national elections as a proxy for exogenous variation in policy uncertainty, we find that policy uncertainty has a negative impact on FDI flows from the U.S. parent firms to their affiliates in 43 countries. Specifically, we document cycles in FDI flows around the timing of elections in both destination countries and the source country. The average FDI rate drops by approximately 12% compared to non-election years, all else equal. The results suggest that the uncertainty related to election outcomes leads economic agents to postpone private investment abroad until some degree of the uncertainty is resolved. The magnitudes of the declines in FDI flows are significantly larger than the effects of policy uncertainty on domestic investment, suggesting that foreign flows of capital are more sensitive to the policy environment, as hypothesized by Dixit (2011). We find that the effect is stronger around elections with close outcomes and in countries with

30

less stable political systems and fewer checks and balances on executive power. Election effects are mitigated when trade openness is large. We also find that the results are robust to the possible endogeneity of election timing as the results are similar for the sample of countries for which the timing of elections is fixed by electoral law.

Two additional findings emerge from the empirical analysis. First, we find that policy uncertainty is not only an emerging market phenomenon. In fact, developed countries in our sample display mild cycles in FDI flows around elections, suggesting that policy uncertainty is important in the developed world as well, although the cycles are more amplified in developing economies. Second, we find that FDI flows, which are considered to be relatively more irreversible than FPI flows, are more sensitive to policy uncertainty than are FPI flows. The difference in sensitivity between relatively irreversible FDI and FPI flows suggests a likely causal link between heightened political uncertainty around election time and declines in FDI flows. Any alternative theory would have to explain not only the reductions in FDI, but also the differential sensitivities of FDI and FPI flows to the election cycle. Among the existing theories, the political uncertainty mechanism best fits the total of our empirical results.

We view our results as having several contributions. First, our results are largely consistent with the implications of various models of direct investment under uncertainty, in particular the Rodrik (1991) model of policy uncertainty and private foreign investment. As far as we know, we are the first to provide evidence of political cycles in FDI flows. Second, we contribute to the literature on the determinants of FDI flows by identifying a political factor that leads to variation in FDI flows over time. Third, our results support the increasing use of election timing as a proxy for variation in political uncertainty. FDI flows are sensitive to the election cycle but FPI flows are not, suggesting that uncertainty is the mechanism underlying the results. Finally, we view our results as contributing to the recent debate over whether policy uncertainty depresses economic activity in general and especially in the wake of the financial

31

crisis. While we do not address the post-crisis recovery directly, our results are suggestive that periods of high uncertainty regarding political outcomes do have real effects.

References

Aguiar, M., and G. Gopinath. 2005. Fire-Sale FDI and Liquidity Crises. Review of Economics and Statistics 87, 439–52.

Albuquerque, R., N. Loayza, and L. Serven. 2005. World Market Integration Through the Lens of Foreign Direct Investors. Journal of International Economics 66, 267–295.

Alesina, A., G. Cohen, and N. Roubini. 1992. Macroeconomic Policy and Elections in OECD Democracies. Economics and Politics 5, 1–30.

Aizenman, J. 2003. Volatility, Employment and the Patterns of FDI in Emerging Markets. Journal of Development Economics 72, 585–601.

Baker, M., C. Foley, and J. Wurgler. 2009. Multinationals as Arbitrageurs: The Effect of Stock Market Valuations on Foreign Direct Investment. Review of Financial Studies 22, 337–369.

Baker, S., N. Bloom, and S. Davis. 2012. Measuring Economic Policy Uncertainty. Working paper, Stanford University.

Bekaert, G., and C. Harvey. 2000. Foreign Speculators and Emerging Equity Markets. Journal of Finance 55, 565–613.

Bekaert, G., C. Harvey, and C. Lundblad. 2006. Growth Volatility and Financial Liberalization. Journal of International Money and Finance 25, 370–403.

Bernanke, B. 1983. Irreversibility, Uncertainty, and Cyclical Investment. Quarterly Journal of Economics, 85–106.

Bernhard, W., and D. Leblang. 2006. Democratic Processes and Financial Markets: Pricing Politics, Cambridge University Press.

Bernhard, W., S. Riley, and P. Vaaler. 2012. How do International Bankers Vote in Developing Country Elections? Working Paper.

Bertaut, C., and L. Pounder. 2009. The Financial Crisis and U.S. Cross-Border Financial Flows. Federal Reserve Bulletin 95, A147–A167.

Bertaut, C., and R. Tryon. 2007. Monthly Estimates of U.S. Cross-Border Securities Positions. International Finance Discussion Papers 910, Board of Governors of the Federal Reserve System (U.S.).

Bhattacharya, U., N. Galpin, and B. Haslem. 2007. The Home Court Advantage in International Corporate Litigation, *Journal of Law and Economics*, 50, 625–659

Bialkowski, J., K. Gottschalk, and T. Wisniewski. 2008. Stock Market Volatility around National Elections. Journal of Banking and Finance 32, 1941–1953.

Blonigen, B. 1997. Firm-Specific Assets and the Link Between Exchange Rates and Foreign Direct Investment. American Economic Review 87, 447–465.

Blonigen, B. 2001. In search of Substitution between Foreign Production and Export. Journal of International Economics 53, 81–104.

Bloom, N., S. Bond, and J. Van Reenen. 2007. Uncertainty and Investment Dynamics. Review of Economic Studies 74, 391–415.

Boutchkova, M., H. Doshi, A. Durnev, and A. Molchanov. 2012. Precarious Politics and Return Volatility. Review of Financial Studies 25, 1111–1154.

Bulan, L. 2005. Real Options, Irreversible Investment and Firm Uncertainty: New Evidence from U.S. Firms. Review of Financial Economics 14, 255–279.

Busse, M., and C. Hefeker. 2007. Political Risk, Institutions and Foreign Direct Investment. European Journal of Political Economy 23, 397–415.

Caballero, R. 1991. On the Sign of the Investment-Uncertainty Relationship. American Economic Review 81, 279-288.

Caballero, R., and M. Hammour. 1998. The Macroeconomics of Specificity. Journal of Political Economy 106, 724–767.

Chen, Y., and M. Funke. 2003. Option Value, Policy Uncertainty, and the Foreign Direct Investment Decision. Hamburg Institute of International Economics discussion paper.

Chuhan, P., S. Claessens, and N. Mamingi. 1998. Equity and Bond Flows to Latin America and Asia: the Role of Global and Country Factors. Journal of Development Economics 55, 439–463.

Colak, G., A. Durnev, and Y. Qian. 2013. Derailed by Political Uncertainty: U.S. Gubernatorial Elections and IPO Activity, Working paper.

Curcuru, S., C. Thomas, F. Warnock, and J. Wongswan. 2011. U.S. International Equity Investment and Past and Prospective Returns. American Economic Review 101, 3440–3455.

Daude, C., and M. Fratzscher. 2008. The Pecking Order of Cross-Border Investment. Journal of International Economics 74, 94–119.

Desai, M., C. Foley, and J. Hines. 2004. A Multinational Perspective on Capital Structure Choice and Internal Capital Markets. Journal of Finance 59, 2451-2488.

Desai, M., C. Foley, and J. Hines. 2006. Capital Controls, Liberalizations, and Foreign Direct Investment. Review of Financial Studies 19, 1433–1464.

Desai, M., C. Foley, and J. Hines. 2008. Capital Structure with Risky Foreign Investment. Journal of Financial Economics 88, 534–553.

Dewenter, K. 1995. Do Exchange Rate Changes Drive Foreign Direct Investment? Journal of Business 68, 405–433.

Dixit, A. 2011. International Trade, Foreign Direct Investment, and Security. Annual Reviews of Economics 3, 191–213 .

Durnev, A. 2010. The Real Effects of Political Uncertainty: Elections and Investment Sensitivity to Stock Prices. Working paper.

Fratzscher, M., and J. Imbs. 2009. Risk Sharing, Finance, and Institutions in International Portfolios. Journal of Financial Economics 94, 428–447.

Froot, K., and J. Stein. 1991. Exchange Rates and Foreign Direct Investment: An Imperfect Capital Markets Approach. Quarterly Journal of Economics 106, 1191–1217.

Gao, P., and Y. Qi. 2013, Political uncertainty and public financing costs: Evidence from U.S. municipal bond markets, working paper.

Giovanni, J., and A. Levchenko. 2009. Trade Openness and Volatility. Review of Economics and Statistics 91, 558-585.

Goldstein, I., and A. Razin. 2006. An Information-Based Trade-Off between Foreign Direct Investment and Foreign Portfolio Investment. Journal of International Economics 70, 271–95.

Griever, W., G. Lee, and F. Warnock. 2001. The U.S. System for Measuring Cross-Border Investment in Securities: A Primer with a Discussion of Recent Developments. Federal Reserve Bulletin, 633–650.

Guiso, L., and G. Parigi. 1999. Investment and Demand Uncertainty. Quarterly Journal of Economics, 185–227.

Hermes, N., and R. Lensink. 2001. Capital Flight and the Uncertainty of Government Policies. Economics Letters 71, 377-381.

Hines, J., and E. Rice. 1994. Fiscal Paradise: Foreign Tax Havens and American Business. Quarterly Journal of Economics 109, 149-182.

Ito, T. 1990. The Timing of Elections and Political Business Cycles in Japan. Journal of Asian Economics 1, 135–156.

Jens, C. 2012. Investment around U.S. Gubernatorial Elections. Working paper, University of Rochester.

Ju, J., and S. Wei. 2010. Domestic Institutions and the Bypass Effect of Financial Globalization. American Economic Journal: Economic Policy 2010, 2(4), 173-204.

Julio, B., and Y. Yook. 2012. Political Uncertainty and Corporate Investment Cycles. Journal of Finance 67, 45–84.

Kim, C., C. Pantzalis, and J.C. Park. 2012, Political Geography and Stock Returns: The Value and Risk Implications of Proximity to Political Power, *Journal of Financial Economics*, 106, 196–228..

Kim, H., and H. Kung. 2013. How Uncertainty Affects Corporate Investment: The Asset Redeployability Channel. Working paper.

Klein, M., and E. Rosengren. 1994. The Real Exchange Rate and Foreign Direct Investment in the United States. Journal of International Economics 36, 373–389.

Krugman, P. 1998. Fire-Sale FDI. Prepared for NBER Conference on Capital Flows to Emerging Markets. mimeo, MIT.

Lipsey, R., and M. Weiss. 1984. Foreign Production and Exports of Individual Firms. Review of Economics and Statistics 66, 304-307.

Markusen, J. 1995. The Boundaries of Multinational Enterprises and the Theory of International Trade. Journal of Economic Perspectives 9, 169-189.

Nordhaus, W. 1975. The Political Business Cycle. Review of Economic Studies 42, 169–190.

Panousi, V., and D. Papanikolaou. 2012. Investment, Idiosyncratic Risk, and Ownership, *Journal of Finance* 67, 1113–1148.

36

Pastor, L., and P. Veronesi. 2013. Political Uncertainty and Risk Premia. Forthcoming em Journal of Financial Economics.

Pindyck, R., and A. Solimano. 1993. Economic Instability and Aggregate Investment. NBER Macroeconomics Annual 8, 259–303.

Rajan, R., and S. Marwah. 1998. The Effects of Policy Uncertainty on the Choice and Timing of Foreign Direct Investment: An Exploratory Firm-Level Assessment. Journal of Economic Development 23, 37–58.

Razin, A., E. Sadka, and C. Yuen. 1998. A Pecking Order of Capital Flows and International Tax Principles. Journal of International Economics 44, 45–68.

Rodrik, D. 1990. How Should Structural Adjustment Programs be Designed? World Development 18, 933–947.

Rodrik, D. 1991. Policy Uncertainty and Private Investment in Developing Countries. Journal of Development Economics 36, 229–242.

Shleifer, A., and R. Vishny. 1992. Liquidation Values and Debt Capacity: A Market Equilibrium Approach. Journal of Finance 47, 1343–66.

Shleifer, A., and R. Vishny. 2003. Stock Market Driven Acquisitions. Journal of Financial Economics 70, 295–311.

Singh, H., and K. Jun. 1995. Some New Evidence on Determinants of Foreign Direct Investment in Developing Countries. The World Bank Policy Research Working Paper 1531.

Thomas, C., F. Warnock, and J. Wongswan. 2004. The Performance of International Portfolios. FRB International Finance Discussion Paper No. 817.

United Nations Conference on Trade And Development (UNCTAD), 2009. World Investment Report 2009: Transnational Corporations, Agricultural Production and Development.

United Nations Conference on Trade And Development (UNCTAD), 2010. World Investment Report 2010 Overview: Investing in a Low-Carbon Economy.

Warnock, F., and C. Cleaver. 2003. Financial Centers and the Geography of Capital Flows. International Finance 6, 27–59.

Warnock, F., and V. Warnock. 2005. International Capital Flows and U.S. Interest Rates. Board of Governors of the Federal Reserve System International Finance Discussion Papers

840.

Wei, S. 1997. Why is Corruption so Much More Taxing than Tax? Arbitrariness Kills. NBER Working Paper 6255.

Wei, S. 2000. How Taxing is Corruption on International Investors. Review of Economics and Statistics 82, 1–11.

Appendix A: Variable Descriptions

Variable	Description
FDI Flows	Quarterly direct investment flows that U.S. parents provide to their foreign affiliates, where a U.S. parent is defined as a U.S. investor of at least 10 percent of a foreign business.
FPI Flows	Monthly net purchases of long-term foreign securities, both debt and equities, by U.S. residents.
$FDI/Total_{jt}$	The ratio of U.S. FDI flow to the recipient country j in a given quarter t to total U.S. FDI flows in quarter $t-1$.
$FDI/Position_{jt}$	The ratio of U.S. FDI flow to the recipient country j in a given quarter t to the cumulative U.S. FDI position in the country j as of the end of quarter $t-1$.
FDI/GDP_{jt}	The ratio of FDI flows to the recipient country j in a given quarter t to the GDP of the country j.
$Election_t$	$Election_t$ takes a value of one if the destination country hold the election in the second half of quarter t or in the first half of quarter $t+1$, and 0 otherwise.
Checks	The number of veto players in a political system, updated annually and taken from the World Bank Database of Political Institutions.
Close	An indicator variable set equal to one if the vote difference is less than the first quartile value, and zero otherwise, where vote difference is defined as the difference between the proportion of the votes garnered by the winner and that received by the runner-up.
Gov. Stability	The government stability index assesses the government's ability to carry out its declared programs, and its ability to stay in office. The index assigns numbers between 1 and 12, where higher values indicate more stable governments. The data are updated on a monthly basis and obtained from International Country Risk Guide (ICRG) produced by Political Risk Services.
Gov. Expenditure	Central government expenses as a percentage of GDP, taken from World Development Indicators provided by the World Bank.
GDP Per Capita	Real Gross Domestic Product per capita, obtained from the World Bank.
GDP Growth	Annual percentage changes in real per capita GDP
GDP Growth Volatility	Standard deviation of growth rate of real per capita GDP over 3 years (years t, t-1, and t-2).
Domestic Market Return	Quarterly returns on a country's market index, calculated using data from Datastream and Bloomberg.
Exchange Rate	Real effective exchange rate between the recipient country's local currency and the U.S. dollar, taken from IMF International Financial Statistics.
Trade Openness	Sum of exports and imports scaled by GDP, where exports and imports data are drawn from the World Bank.

Table 1
Capital Flows Summary Statistics

This table report the annualized cross-border flows of capital (unit: $ millions) averaged by country. The first column shows average foreign direct investment (FDI) flows per year from U.S. to each of the 43 recipient countries. The next column presents foreign portfolio equity investment (FPEI) flows from the U.S. to each of the 44 countries. The final column report foreign portfolio debt investment (FPDI) from the U.S. to each of the 44 countries. Panel B provides summary statistics for various measures of capital flows. The first two rows summarize raw FDI flows as well as of the three measures of FDI flows. The next two rows report the results for FPEI flows and the final two rows report the results for FPDI flows. See the Appendix for variable descriptions as well as the variable sources.

Panel A: Annualized Flows Averaged by Country

Country	FDI	FPEI	FPDI	Country	FDI	FPEI	FPDI
Argentina	1,152.6	113.1	32.7	Malaysia	825.5	403.7	254.3
Australia	4,295.6	504.5	6,029.6	Mexico	6,513.9	-428.7	862.8
Austria	235.2	33.8	-683.4	Netherlands	24,481.8	-652.2	-250.6
Belgium	3,333.8	-297.0	18,468.1	New Zealand	170.7	8.3	2,668.8
Brazil	3,314.8	4,788.4	988.7	Norway	537.8	-365.9	51.8
Canada	13,892.8	5,874.7	6,145.8	Pakistan	.	54.2	54.1
Chile	1,470.1	65.5	24.7	Peru	378.9	74.5	79.1
Colombia	495.1	31.2	694.0	Philippines	71.8	122.1	719.9
Czech Republic	236.8	-43.1	-25.2	Poland	438.8	74.8	117.7
Denmark	447.7	197.4	-491.1	Portugal	196.5	155.5	317.5
Finland	177.8	47.8	313.4	Russia	1,041.2	30.8	-179.3
France	3,368.4	3,146.6	-1,036.6	Singapore	4,935.2	310.5	-2,428.9
Germany	4,828.8	3,538.4	-4,377.8	South Africa	376.5	460.4	410.5
Greece	65.0	82.4	-346.6	South Korea	1,684.7	1,623.7	666.9
Hungary	570.5	8.8	-107.3	Spain	2,327.5	585.5	-787.1
India	1,011.3	703.1	344.8	Sweden	640.7	-160.8	211.4
Indonesia	811.1	247.6	387.9	Switzerland	6,679.7	614.8	948.2
Ireland	7,818.2	-38.7	1,212.5	Taiwan	905.4	2,811.2	-227.8
Israel	854.4	753.7	373.7	Thailand	715.7	178.6	87.9
Italy	2,141.1	139.4	-1,957.4	Turkey	450.9	307.7	313.5
Japan	4,287.9	12,402.9	-1,448.6	United Kingdom	24,192.1	24,834.4	18,764.1
Luxembourg	6,867.4	-532.1	19,241.2	Venezuela	885.8	60.4	802.2

(continued)

Table 1–*Continued*

	Flow ($ millions)	Flow/GDP	Flow/Position	$ln(Flow + \sqrt{(Flow^2 + 1)})$
Panel B: Summary Statistics (Annualized Flows)				
FDI				
Mean	3,355.3	1.13%	13.00%	6.00
Standard Deviation	7,795.6	4.18%	2.02%	5.10
FPEI				
Mean	1,485.3	0.15%	3.08%	2.25
Standard Deviation	6,502.9	0.72%	17.41%	6.67
FPDI				
Mean	1,132.7	0.61%	8.11%	0.06
Standard Deviation	8,590.1	5.85%	92.93%	7.27

Table 2
Election Summary Statistics

Panel A reports summary statistics for 184 national elections held between 1994 and 2010 in the 45 sample countries including the U.S. Panel B summarizes various characteristics of 44 destination countries. See the Appendix for variable descriptions as well as the variable sources.

Panel A: Election Characteristics			
	Mean	Median	St.Dev.
Election Frequency (unit: quarters)	16.4	16.0	2.3
Length of Term (unit: years)	4.4	4.0	0.7
Percent of Votes Won in an Election			
Winner (%)	41.7	40.0	14.2
Runner-up (%)	28.6	27.0	10.1
Third place (%)	11.5	11.4	5.5
Type of Elections			
Legislative (%)	73.6		
Presidential (%)	26.4		
Proportion of Elections with Exogenous Timing (%)	45.3		
Change of Government Head (%)	56.4		
Change of Ruling Party (%)	48.9		
Panel B: Destination Country Characteristics			
Checks and Balances	4.06	4.00	1.92
ICRG Government Stability Rating	7.82	8.00	2.01
Government Consumption/GDP	0.16	0.15	0.06
GDP Per Capita ($US)	9,183.1	3,273.1	12,842.1
GDP Growth	0.078	0.077	0.130
Stock Market Return (Monthly)	0.010	0.012	0.078
Change in Exchange Rate (Monthly)	0.003	0.000	0.117
Trade Openness	0.789	0.626	0.586

Table 3
FDI Flows around Elections

This table reports estimates of the following specification:

$$FDI_{jt} = \gamma_j + \delta_t + \sum_{k=-2}^{2} \beta_k Election_{j,t+k} + \varepsilon_{jt},$$

The dependent variable, FDI, is measured in four ways. $Flow/Position$ is the U.S. FDI flow to a recipient country in a given quarter scaled by the U.S. FDI position in that country at the end of the previous quarter. $Flow/Total$ is defined as the U.S. FDI flow to recipient country j in a given quarter as a proportion of total U.S. FDI flows around the world at the end of the previous quarter. $Flow/GDP$ is the U.S. FDI flow to a recipient country in a given quarter scaled by the lagged GDP of the country. The final measure is a sign-preserving log transformation used by Busse and Hefeker (2007). $Election$ is set equal to one if the recipient country under consideration holds a national election in the second half of the given quarter or in the first half of the next quarter, and zero otherwise. See appendix for detailed variable descriptions. Country and time (quarterly frequency) fixed effects are included. Standard errors are clustered at the country level and the corresponding t-statistics are reported in brackets.

	FDI/Position	FDI/Total	FDI/GDP	$ln(FDI + \sqrt{(FDI^2+1)})$
Election$_{t-2}$	0.0012	0.0014	0.0013	0.3302
	[0.542]	[0.609]	[0.356]	[0.841]
Election$_{t-1}$	-0.0118*	-0.0035*	-0.0052	-0.1369
	[1.701]	[-1.760]	[1.193]	[0.279]
Election$_t$	-0.0155***	-0.0088***	-0.018**	-0.4434**
	[-3.520]	[-3.256]	[-2.446]	[-2.080]
Election$_{t+1}$	0.0147	0.0060	0.0037	0.1564
	[1.484]	[1.195]	[0.895]	[1.117]
Election$_{t+2}$	0.0023	0.0032	-0.0110	-0.0625
	[0.221]	[1.107]	[-0.658]	[-0.123]
Constant	0.0253***	0.0126***	-0.0020	5.7530***
	[2.719]	[4.225]	[-0.072]	[11.307]
Observations	2,512	2,802	2,802	2,802
Adj. R^2	0.184	0.298	0.304	0.164

Table 4
FDI Regressions: Country Controls

This table reports estimates of the following specification:

$$FDI_{jt} = \gamma_j + \delta_t + \sum_{k=-2}^{2} \beta_k Election_{j,t+k} + \mathbf{X}'\theta + \varepsilon_{\mathbf{jt}},$$

where j indexes country and t indexes time. X is a vector of control variables including government stability, GDP per capita, GDP growth, growth volatility, government expenditures to GDP, lagged stock market return, stock return volatility, exchange rates, exchange rate volatility, and trade openness. Each column reports the estimates from the regression with different transformations of FDI flows. $Election$ is set equal to one if the country under consideration holds a national election in the second half of the given quarter or in the first half of the next quarter, and zero otherwise. The coefficients for $Election_{t-2}$ and $Election_{t+2}$ are not reported to save space. See appendix for detailed variable descriptions. Country and time (quarterly frequency) fixed effects are included. Standard errors are clustered at the country level and the corresponding t-statistics are reported in brackets.

	FDI/Position	FDI/Total	FDI/GDP	$ln(FDI + \sqrt{(FDI^2 + 1)})$
Election$_{t-1}$	-0.0124	-0.0033*	-0.0047	-0.0969
	[-1.520]	[-1.604]	[1.126]	[0.253]
Election$_t$	-0.0146***	-0.0090***	-0.0177**	-0.4211*
	[-2.908]	[-2.956]	[-2.293]	[-1.086]
Election$_{t+1}$	0.0118	.0062	0.0031	0.1428
	[1.195]	[1.024]	[0.866]	[0.979]
Government Stability	0.0006	-0.0002	0.0034	0.3113**
	[0.301]	[-0.129]	[1.405]	[2.705]
GDP Per Capita	-0.0000	0.0000**	0.0000***	-0.0000
	[-0.479]	[2.084]	[2.849]	[-0.163]
GDP Growth	0.1158***	0.0184**	0.1057*	4.9200***
	[5.264]	[2.448]	[1.727]	[4.048]
GDP Growth Volatility	0.0057	-0.0616	-0.0740*	-4.101**
	[0.442]	[-0.969]	[-1.794]	[-2.117]
Government Expenditures/GDP	0.0026**	0.0021	0.0745	0.0299
	[2.451]	[1.026]	[1.266]	[0.203]
Domestic Market Return	0.0015**	-0.0001	-0.0002	0.0364
	[2.082]	[-0.776]	[-0.170]	[1.172]
Return Volatility	-0.0008	0.0001	-0.0007*	-0.0234
'	[-0.857]	[0.578]	[-1.748]	[-0.661]
Δ Exchange Rate	-0.0113	-0.0006	0.0037	-0.8851
	[-0.437]	[-0.171]	[0.279]	[-1.430]
Exchange Rate Volatility	0.0000	0.0000	0.0000	0.0001
	[1.555]	[0.215]	[1.316]	[0.535]
Trade Openness	0.0002	0.0002	0.0028**	0.0306**
	[1.424]	[1.633]	[2.300]	[2.684]
Observations	1,800	1,928	1,928	1,928
Adj. R^2	0.194	0.244	0.347	0.169

Table 5
FDI Regressions: Including U.S. Elections

This table reports estimates of the following specification:

$$FDI_{jt} = \gamma_j + \delta_t + \sum_{k=-2}^{2} \beta_k Election_{j,t+k} + \sum_{l=-2}^{2} \delta_l Election_{US,t+l} + X'\theta + \varepsilon_{jt}$$

where j indexes country and t indexes time. X is a vector of control variables including government stability, GDP per capita, GDP growth, growth volatility, government expenditures to GDP, lagged stock market return, stock return volatility, exchange rates, exchange rate volatility, and trade openness. Each column reports the estimates from the regression with different transformations of FDI flows. *Election* is set equal to one if the country under consideration holds a national election in the second half of the given quarter or in the first half of the next quarter, and zero otherwise. The coefficients for the control variables and the election dummies for $t \pm 2$ are not reported to save space. See appendix for detailed variable descriptions. Country and year fixed effects are included. Standard errors are clustered at the country level and the corresponding t-statistics are reported in brackets.

	FDI/Position	FDI/Total	FDI/GDP	$ln(FDI + \sqrt{(FDI^2 + 1)})$
Election$_{t-1}$	-0.0103*	-0.0050*	-0.0038	-0.1527
	[-1.741]	[-1.999]	[-1.100]	[-0.253]
Election$_t$	-0.0156***	-0.0089***	0.0140**	-0.4692**
	[-3.541]	[-3.228]	[2.324]	[-2.029]
Election$_{t+1}$	0.0136	0.0054*	0.0037	0.1507
	[0.486]	[1.694]	[0.080]	[0.107]
US Election$_{t-1}$	-0.0168**	0.0000	-0.0124*	-1.1540*
	[-2.393]	[0.006]	[-1.767]	[-1.748]
US Election$_t$	-0.0147***	-0.0054***	-0.0405***	-1.9882***
	[-2.916]	[-2.699]	[-2.690]	[-3.137]
US Election$_{t+1}$	0.0366**	-0.0000	0.0249*	1.2502**
	[2.218]	[-0.005]	[1.850]	[2.043]
Observations	1,800	1,928	1,928	1,928
Adj. R^2	0.144	0.238	0.332	0.134

Table 6
FDI Regressions: Exogenous Timing of Elections

This table reports estimates of the following specification:

$$FDI_{jt} = \gamma_j + \delta_t + \sum_{k=-2}^{2} \beta_k Election_{j,t+k} + X'\theta + \varepsilon_{jt}$$

where j indexes country and t indexes time. X is a vector of control variables including government stability, GDP per capita, GDP growth, growth volatility, government expenditures to GDP, lagged stock market return, stock return volatility, exchange rates, exchange rate volatility, and trade openness. Each column reports the estimates from the regression with different transformations of FDI flows. The analysis considers the subsample of countries with fixed election timing only. *Election* is set equal to one if the country under consideration holds a national election in the second half of the given quarter or in the first half of the next quarter, and zero otherwise. See appendix for detailed variable descriptions. Country and year/quarter fixed effects are included. Standard errors are clustered at the country level and the corresponding t-statistics are reported in brackets.

	(1)	(2)	(3)	(4)
	FDI/Position	FDI/Total	FDI/GDP	$ln(FDI + \sqrt{(FDI^2 + 1)})$
$Election_{t-1}$	-0.0041	-0.0054	-0.3362	-0.0634
	[-1.109]	[-1.459]	[-0.826]	[-1.142]
$Election_t$	-0.0124**	-0.0110**	-1.1085*	-0.4949*
	[-2.202]	[-2.103]	[-1.815]	[-1.892]
$Election_{t+1}$	0.0048*	0.0053	0.2586	0.1068
	[1.825]	[0.798]	[0.624]	[0.283]
Observations	764	712	764	764
Adj. R^2	0.284	0.189	0.310	0.170

Table 7
FDI Flows around Close Elections

This table reports estimates of the following specification:

$$\frac{FDI_{jt}}{Position_{j,t-1}} = \gamma_j + \delta_t + \alpha_1 \cdot Close_{jt} + \alpha_2 \cdot Wide_{jt} + \sum_{k=-2}^{2} \beta_k Election_{j,t+k} + \mathbf{X'}\theta + \varepsilon_{jt},$$

where j indexes country and t indexes time. *Close* is a dummy variable equal to one if the margin of victory for a given election is in the lowest quartile of the margin of victor distribution. *Wide* is a dummy variable equal to one if the margin of victory for a given election is in the highest quartile of the margin of victor distribution. X is a vector of control variables including government stability, GDP per capita, GDP growth, growth volatility, government expenditures to GDP, lagged stock market return, stock return volatility, exchange rates, exchange rate volatility, and trade openness. Each column reports the estimates from the regression with different transformations of FDI flows.. *Election* is set equal to one if the country under consideration holds a national election in the second half of the given quarter or in the first half of the next quarter, and zero otherwise. See appendix for detailed variable descriptions. The first two columns report the results for the full sample and the final two columns report results for the sample of countries with exogenous election timing. Country and year/quarter fixed effects are included. Standard errors are clustered at the country level and the corresponding t-statistics are reported in brackets.

	Full Sample		Exogenous Timing Sample	
Election$_{t-1}$	-0.0099*	-0.0100*	-0.0042	-0.0042
	[-1.737]	[-1.739]	[-1.101]	[-1.109]
Election$_t$	-0.0052*	-0.0049*	-0.0077*	-0.0075*
	[-1.701]	[-1.708]	[-1.702]	[-1.698]
Close Election Interaction	-0.0096**	-0.0099**	-0.0108*	-0.0112*
	[-2.552]	[-2.547]	[-1.922]	[-1.926]
Wide Margin of Victory Interaction		0.0062		0.0089
		[1.191]		[0.996]
Election$_{t+1}$	0.0116	0.0118	0.0048*	0.0047*
	[0.587]	[0.588]	[1.827]	[1.822]
Observations	1,800	1,800	764	764
Adj. R^2	0.155	0.162	0.290	0.297

Table 8
Interactions with Measures of Government Stability

This table reports estimates of the following specification:

$$\frac{FDI_{jt}}{Position_{j,t-1}} = \gamma_j + \delta_t + \alpha_1 \cdot Z_{jt} + \alpha_2 \cdot Z_{jt} \cdot Election_{jt} + \sum_{k=-2}^{2} \beta_k Election_{j,t+k} + \mathbf{X}'\theta + \varepsilon_{jt},$$

where Z_{jt} is a time-varying country characteristic meant to capture differences in the propensity for large policy changes after elections. Four measures of Z are utilized: ICRG government stability ratings, checks and balances on executive authority, World Bank classification of high income countries, and a dummy variable indicating whether a country's trade openness is above the median in a given year across countries. X is a vector of control variables including government stability, GDP per capita, GDP growth, growth volatility, government expenditures to GDP, lagged stock market return, stock return volatility, exchange rates, exchange rate volatility, and trade openness. $Election$ is set equal to one if the country under consideration holds a national election in the second half of the given quarter or in the first half of the next quarter, and zero otherwise. See appendix for detailed variable descriptions. Country and time (quarterly frequency) fixed effects are included. Standard errors are clustered at the country level and the corresponding t-statistics are reported in brackets.

	(1)	(2)	(3)	(4)
	Govt. Stability	Checks & Balances	High Income	Trade Openness
$Election_t$	-0.0103***	-0.0066**	-0.0232***	-0.0231***
	[-2.955]	[-2.129]	[-2.840]	[-3.321]
Stability × $Election_t$	0.0022*			
	[1.950]			
Checks × $Election_t$		0.0017		
		[1.591]		
High Income × $Election_t$			0.0119	
			[1.022]	
High Openness × $Election_t$				0.0206**
				[2.183]
Observations	1,800	1,800	1,800	1,800
Adj. R^2	0.145	0.145	0.146	0.146

Table 9
Election Cycles and World Portfolio Investment Flows

This table reports seemingly unrelated regression estimates for the following equations:

$$\frac{FDI_{jt}}{Position_{j,t-1}} = \gamma_j + \delta_t + \sum_{k=-2}^{2} \beta_k Election_{j,t+k} + X'\theta + \varepsilon_{jt}$$

$$\frac{FPI_{jt}}{Position_{j,t-1}} = \gamma'_j + \delta'_t + \sum_{k=-2}^{2} \beta'_k Election_{j,t+k} + X'\eta + \nu_{jt},$$

where FPI represents foreign portfolio equity investment (FPEI) flows, foreign portfolio debt investment (FPDI) flows, or the sum of the two flows. We employ the flows/position measure as the dependent variable. X is a vector of control variables, which includes a recipient country's GDP growth, GDP per capita, volatility of GDP growth, government consumption scaled by GDP, lagged, lead, and contemporaneous stock market return, stock market volatility, the U.S. market return, change in exchange rate, volatility of exchange rates, and trade openness. See appendix for detailed variable descriptions. Country and time (quarterly frequency) fixed effects are included. Standard errors are clustered at the country level and the corresponding t-statistics are reported in brackets.

	FDI	Equity FPI	Debt FPI	Total FPI
Election$_{t-1}$	-0.0075	-0.0004	0.0250	-0.0022
	[-1.170]	[-0.056]	[0.236]	[-0.349]
Election$_t$	-0.0172***	0.0019	-0.0073	0.0009
	[-2.831]	[0.287]	[-0.203]	[0.149]
Election$_{+1}$	0.0069	-0.0045	-0.1321	0.0021
	[1.009]	[-0.772]	[-1.450]	[0.388]
Observations	1,649	1,649	1,649	1,649
Adj. R^2	0.223	0.084	0.066	0.203
Test: ($\beta_{FDI} - \beta_{FPI} = 0$)				
Difference		-0.0191***	-0.0099**	-0.0181***
		[-3.56]	[2.45]	[-3.19]

49